DARE TO
BELIEVE

BY MARK SHARP

Published by
Xulon Press
11350 Random Hills Road
Suite 800
Fairfax, VA 22030
(703) 279-6511
XulonPress.com

To order additional copies, call 1-866-909-BOOK (2665).

Foreword

Most people start out their lives with a set of hopes and dreams for the future. They hope that they will become famous, or maybe live in a beautiful house by the ocean, or break some world athletic record.

Unfortunately, as life progresses, many see their dreams slip away.

What is it about our expectations that shapes the way we live our lives? Could it be that what we want is not what we need? Could it be that there is something going on that is bigger than us? Do the choices we make have consequences?

In many ways life is like a game; not one to be taken lightly, but still a game. It involves a lot of complicated strategy, and can be very difficult at times. We are not offered the choice to play; everyone who is born—plays.

I was very optimistic about the future when I was younger. I expected to be blessed in such categories as athletics, marriage, kids, career, and anything else I decided on later. I excluded any plans that included doctors. I especially excluded doctors bearing bad news like, "You have an incurable disease that will wipe out the neurotransmitters in your brain." Why would anyone include an event like that in his or her plans?

One thing we all have in common is that we have a life to live and choices to make. I hope that Dare to Believe will provide some direction to you as you face the task of managing those choices.

Mark Sharp
May 2002

Dedications

When you look back on your life, certain people and events stand out as significant. I have been very fortunate to be around the kind of people that stay and don't leave. As this book demonstrates, it is a far-from-perfect world we live in, but the people I want to mention here are people who have been patient and helpful to me in special ways, despite my many imperfections. To anyone who prayed for me, or to anyone that I do not mention, I want to say "thank-you" also.

The first thanks must to go to my wife, Kelly, who has had to face more difficulties and disappointments than I will ever know. She has been forced to give up on the dream of a perfect life and has had to carry a burden daily that is more than she deserves. Kelly and I spoke at a Valentine banquet. We both prepared our talks, and then we compared notes to see how the talk would fit together. She was going to describe how she had to pick up a lot of the work at home that I could not do. At that time I selfishly asked her to edit that part out, using the excuse that it made me look bad. Therefore, to correct my mistake, I want everyone to know that her statements were valid and continue to be valid. And for those of you who have spouses who are battling difficult health problems, I honor you for your courage to stay and make the sacrifices that are necessary!

I also want to thank my parents, who have been encouraging throughout this whole ordeal. They found people to pray for me that I did not even know. They provided rides, watched the kids, and helped out in many other ways.

I also thank my sons Jeremy, Jordan, and Jesse, who have virtually ignored my sometimes-embarrassing appearance. They have not treated me any differently than they would anyone else, and that is the greatest compliment that they could give me.

As I mention in this book, I thank my father-in-law for making sure that I made it to surgery, and all my family for being so supportive.

Winona Lake Grace Brethren Church: how do you thank a group that has done such a good job of communicating their concern and care during this time? You have believed in me. I only hope that I can learn from your great example. Thanks to the pastor and staff for your continued support. I also want to thank the people in our Bible study group, who have been with me from the beginning.

Lastly, I give thanks to the incredible neurological staff at Cleveland Clinic. Your hard work and commitment have resulted in at least one life that has been drastically changed. There is no way to properly thank you for the opportunity that you have given to me. You gave me a new chance to live.

The Sharp family (clockwise): Mark (upper left), Jeremy, Jesse, Kelly and Jordan.

Table of Contents

Chapter 1

The Game

It's the final game of the season. The most dominating pitcher in the league is pitching to the opponent's smallest batter, who hasn't been on base all season. The home team trails by one with a runner on first. The batter has swung twice and missed. This little league game appears to be over.

The pitcher throws what he expects to be strike three.

The batter swings at what the crowd expects to be strike three.

The bat makes contact. It travels high over the center fielder's head.

The center fielder stretches for the ball. Back...back...back—he falls to the ground. Lying there, he reaches up. The ball smacks his mitt. The game is over.

A dramatic ending—not what anyone would have predicted. That's the way life is, too. We think we have it all figured out; we think we can win. But the unexpected can happen at any moment.

Each of us was brought into this game called "life" without being asked. To make matters worse, we didn't start out knowing all the rules for playing. Maybe someone explained some of the rules to us, but how do we know for sure that *they* understood the game? Where did *they* learn the rules? Everyone seems to have a different idea of how the game should be played.

This game is the adventure of all adventures.

You are playing the game of Life. You are finding that this game is the adventure of all adventures. It requires strategy, decision-making, insight, and, most of all, endurance. The stakes are high.

Do you want to play well? Are you even sure that you know what it takes to play well?

This

is your personal invitation

to learn the secrets

of the game of Life.

A manual

will be provided.

Your instructor

will be

the creator of the game

himself.

Although this invitation is open to all players, many will refuse it. Some will think it's a hoax. To others it will seem like it requires too much effort. Some won't like the rules, so they will choose to play their own way, ignoring the fact that they are losing.

But a few will take a serious look at this invitation and decide to find out more. If you are one of them, keep reading.

Chapter 2

The Basics of the Game

Welcome! You have chosen to find out more about the game called Life. The game begins with some basic ground rules:

Rule Number One: You may only play this game once. If you lose the game you lose anything acquired during the game—and more.

Rule Number Two: In order to be successful, participants are required to navigate the terrain provided to them and find the path that leads to the winning finish area.

Rule Number Three: Everyone's playing field will be different, unique to that person. It will be based on the strength and weaknesses of the player. The creator of the game will determine this.

How The Game is Played:

1. The game's creator has provided someone as a guide to assist you. The guide knows the way to the winning finish line. This guide is yours for the duration of the game. He can provide instruction and give you extra strength and insight. You will need to listen carefully to what he says, however, because he speaks very softly. Keep in mind that he will only tell you the correct route if you ask him to do so.
2. You have the option of traveling based on information from your guide, or you can take advantage of the freedom offered you to make your own decisions.
3. In addition to the guide provided, you will encounter an opponent posing as a second guide. He will offer you information, but be careful—he only knows the way to the losing finish area. You don't even have to ask him for directions; he will most likely approach you with his guidance. His information

will make a lot of sense to you. He will typically have an easier route or a faster plan. But remember where he is taking you; he only knows how to lose.

4. You will be provided with a rule book. This will also be critical to your chances for winning the game. It has been written by the game's creator. It is quite comprehensive, and will require careful study to understand. The more you study, the more prepared you will be for the journey.

Clues and cautions for players of the game:

People who have played the game have reported experiencing a wide array of emotions while playing, from incredible joy to bitter agony.

Statistics show that most people playing this game lose! Remember—losers will lose *everything*! This game *must* be taken seriously.

A helpful clue has been given out by the game's creator: in order to find the winning area you must chose the guide which he has provided. Without him no player has found, or ever will find, the winning area.

The game's creator retains the right to end the game for any player, or for all players, at any time. At the end of the game player's scores will be evaluated. All final judgments will be at the discretion of the creator.

Does this sound like the game you're in? Are you willing to accept help to get to the winning finish line? Keep reading.

Chapter 3
Count Me In!

I am a fellow participant in this exciting, challenging game. Recently, for me, the game has moved to a higher level of difficulty—more difficult than I could have ever predicted. The challenge began when I was about 30. First, my left wrist started giving me trouble. My doctor recommended that I go to an orthopedic surgeon. The surgeon thought it was a carpal tunnel problem and recommended surgery. The surgery helped the pain, but I never regained use of the wrist.

Then my family doctor noticed that my left leg had stopped working properly. I could run as fast as normal, but I could not walk. This time my family doctor sent me to a neurologist. The neurologist just looked at me and, I think, could tell what was going on. But he did a brain scan to confirm it.

When I went back after the brain scan, he came breezing into the room where I was waiting with my wife Kelly and with Jesse, the youngest of our three sons. "You have Parkinsonism," he told me bluntly. He didn't explain what it was, or give a prognosis. He just wrote a prescription and said, "This should control it. Take care."

Basically, all we knew about Parkinson's disease was that my uncle had it and it affected his motor skills. Kelly and I looked it up in the encyclopedia, and I remember reading that it wasn't life-threatening. "Good," I thought, "I'll be here for my family as the boys grow up." I was a little apprehensive, however, because it said that your last days would be pretty uncomfortable. I had no idea at that time how much Parkinson's would change my life. I was born optimistic, and to this point I have never felt that this disease has beaten me or is too big for God to handle. But the condition known as Parkinson's disease described in this book has been merciless.

Somehow, though, life goes on. History keeps being made. The lawn needs to be mowed. The kids are late for baseball practice. The board meeting lasted three hours last night. The sum of the bills is greater than the current checking balance. The dog needs to be let out. The kids take turns giving reasons why they do not like the supper menu.

In the routine of living our lives, it is sometimes hard to believe that there is a great divine plan unfolding.

In the routine of living our lives, it is sometimes hard to believe that there is a great divine plan unfolding. Even harder to believe is that we have any part in it—or that we could have any effect on the plan, one way or another.

You can use any literary device available to describe life, but you are still left with only two options when attempting to understand it.

Option One: Close your eyes and pretend that God is not responsible for what goes on, or that He does not exist.

The problem with this approach is that closing your eyes will cause you to trip and fall, hurting yourself and those around you.

Option Two: Choose to pursue the God who Is, Was, and Will be.

Accept the fact that whether we like the life He has given us or not, we are in no position to bargain. He holds the keys that no man on earth has ever been able to find on his own—the keys to a life that will never end.

Since my diagnosis, God has continued to bless me, giving me a wonderful home, a good job, and a family to love. But even if He had not, and even if a cure for Parkinson's is delayed, God is still God and the game is still on.

Maybe life seems to be just a game, and you cannot really believe in this God that no one can see. But at least stop and consider the risks of not choosing to believe. You can go ahead and refuse to investigate His claims. You can live like everybody else. You can make your own decisions.

Still, in the end, you will either win or lose. But if you do nothing, you're certain to lose. That's why I've chosen to say, "Count me in!"

Chapter 4

Joining the Team

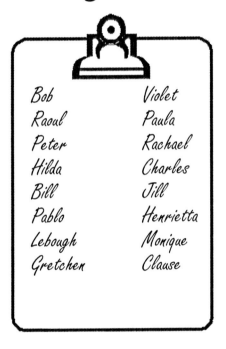

Bob	Violet
Raoul	Paula
Peter	Rachael
Hilda	Charles
Bill	Jill
Pablo	Henrietta
Lebough	Monique
Gretchen	Clause

In the past I have been responsible for creating lists of names which would indicate whether someone made an athletic team. These are very difficult decisions, especially when you watch little hearts break as they parade past the list.

God is making a list. There will be a lot of broken hearts when people find that their name is not on that list.

You may think that you don't need or want to be on God's team. You may not think that you are good enough to make the team. Or maybe, when you think of God, you think of a coach who screams and disciplines—a perfectionistic superior who stands aloof and distant. These are legitimate concerns. If these facts about God were true, this would not be a team worth being on.

I do not claim to be a theologian, although I have had a number of classes on theology. I do not talk to God nearly as often as I should. I cannot say that I have always agreed with Him on how His plan is played out. But what I do know is that despite my lack of faith in Him, He continues to remain with me. I see His hand in my life in big ways and in small ones. He promised that He would never leave us or forsake us. When I don't understand what He is doing, I only need to look back at how many times He has come to my rescue.

When I don't understand what He is doing, I only need to look back at how many times He has come to my rescue.

For example, at the time of my diagnosis, I was a supervisor at a local orthopedic company. Previous to my illness, I was able to work an entire day without thinking about pain and discomfort, or wondering whether I was going to be able to get up and walk after sitting at a meeting.

Shortly after the diagnosis my job was eliminated due to "reorganization." I suspected that it had something to do with my diagnosis (although I asked a lawyer friend of mine and he said that I did not have a case). A year later my job came up again on the company's Intranet. I applied and suddenly the job was not open any more. The crazy thing was that in my former job the areas that I had supervised had increased over 100% in production!

Whether my exclusion was intentional or an oversight, I was sent out to find a job while struggling with a major disability. Living with a disability makes competing in the job market difficult. Companies who have employees who become disabled while employed should have some responsibility toward those employees. In my case, however, while I was put in a very awkward position, the corporation went on to continue its profitable ways.

Over the next two years I probably went to twenty-five or thirty interviews. To prepare for the interviews, I would find out as much as I could about the company, writing down the names and phone numbers of references. I would dress appropriately, take my medication at just the right time, then hope that my body would cooperate at the interview. Many times I left the interview feeling confident that I had been the most qualified candidate, but never heard back from the prospective employer.

One company gave me a job for thirty days, with the guarantee that I would be hired at the end. I worked very hard for the company. I was asked to teach a class on integrity to a group of employees that I was managing. Soon after I taught the class, I learned that although the company promoted integrity, they did not practice it. At the end of the thirty days I was required to take part in an all-day interview, competing with healthy engineers. We had no breaks, even for lunch; there was no time to take my medication. I lost the competition. Since I had not asked for a break, I had no case—I had no right to ask for another chance.

I took a job in Archibald, Ohio, for a few months, but my house would not sell and my family could not come to join me.

When a friend asked me to work on a consultant basis back in Warsaw, I took the chance. Thanks to his assistance and to the director of the Research and Development department, a huge need was met for our family. I worked for two years with consultant status, waiting for a full-time position to open. After the two years I experienced my second corporate reorganization. A large pharmaceutical firm bought our company. This time, instead of losing a job, I was hired. The man who hired me relocated in Warsaw just long enough to hire me, then moved back to Pennsylvania.

In the meantime, the company that I had left in Ohio went out of business.

God was busy taking care of me and my family. Worrying would not have helped, but believing in God did. And having a lot of people asking God to take care of us didn't hurt, either.

Now I work for a company that is a competitor to the orthopedic company that I first worked for. My current employer has not only given me a job, but also, when my medicine isn't working, I can go home, lie down until I feel better, and then come back. Sometimes I have needed to do this up to three times a day in order to get in my full eight hours of work. I want to thank DePuy, a division of

Johnson and Johnson, for believing that I could become an effective employee. In particular I want to thank Don McNulty and Todd Smith, respectively manager and director of the Research and Development department, and Bob Richard, who actually hired me.

As I mentioned earlier, working was far from easy. There were times when Dave Warner, a co-worker, would have to find a cart for me to push to the door because my blood pressure had dropped so low that I could not walk, or even hold my head up to work at a computer. There were times when I could not even make it to the door with the cart, and just had to suffer through it.

In one instance I had to travel for a vendor. Due to flight pressure or something, I had a very bad spell. It was really ugly. The management of the company did not understand what was happening to me (neither did I), but they were very gracious. That was the only time I had to be in a wheelchair. I learned that people in airports treat you differently when you are being wheeled through the terminal.

Like any good coach, God does ask a lot of us. I sometimes feel overwhelmed with the responsibilities of being a father, a husband, an employee, and a Christian, trying to function in a normal world with a body that won't always cooperate.

I sometimes feel overwhelmed trying to function in a normal world with a body that won't always cooperate.

In the Old Testament, God called Jeremiah to prophesy for Him. Jeremiah obeyed. It was not long until the job of prophesying got difficult. Jeremiah came to God and brought his complaint. God's answer indicates the kind of expectations He has for us. God asked Jeremiah, " If you have raced with men and they have worn you out, how can you compete with horses? (Jeremiah 12:5)

Do you ever feel that way—that you just can't keep up? Yet God expects us to faithfully do what He has called us to do. The good news, though, is that God continued His conversation with Jeremiah by encouraging and strengthening him (and assuring him that He would be with him).

Yes, there is a great cost in following God, but He is the kind of coach who seems to have a way of giving you help and encouragement just when you really need it. Sometimes you realize that He prepared that encouragement far ahead of time.

For example, when I was eight years old I attended a Bible school class that our pastor was teaching. He spoke about heaven and hell, explaining that God sent Jesus to pay the price for my sins so I could avoid hell and go to heaven. As a young boy I did not understand heaven, but I was observant enough to realize that hell was a place that I didn't want to go. That day I decided to join God's team by accepting His sacrifice. At that time it seemed rather insignificant. Although the angels were rejoicing, I could not hear them. No band played; it was just something that happened.

Some years later, during my freshman year in high school, my grandparents were killed in a car accident. I struggled a lot over the loss of such special people in my life. When we were packing up their belongings, I came across Grandma's devotion book. I turned to a page that had been marked with her distinctive handwriting. "Today Mark asked Jesus into his life," it said.

Did I just "happen" to turn to that page? Did Grandma ever think that I would see that page when she wrote it?

God cared about a high school kid who had just lost his grandparents to a car accident. God, knowing the future, prearranged years in advance for Grandma to write the encouragement that I would need that day. Then He arranged for me to turn to just the right page.

God wants us to join His team—He knows what He can make of us. He is trying to communicate His plan to us. Yet we often accuse Him of being hard to reach. We need to realize that the distance between God and us comes from us moving away, not Him. The mess this world is in is our fault, not His. In fact, God has gone on record as saying that He deeply cares for us. He also recorded the words that you often see held up during football games: John 3:16. The verse says, "For God so loved the world that he gave his one and only Son, so that whoever believes in him shall not perish but have eternal life." The announcers typically make fun of the sign, but it doesn't change the truth that God loves! The amazing thing is that He not only says that He loves us, but He proved it by sending His Son to die in our place, bearing the punishment for our sins.

I want to be very sensitive here. I understand that making a commitment to follow God is a very serious matter. It involves a whole new way of thinking about life. My life no longer belongs to me—He now controls it.

The distance between God and us comes from us moving away, not Him.

When I was choosing a specialist to treat my Parkinson's disease, I wanted the best that I could get. After all, I was trusting him with the only life that I have. It was a scary decision to make.

You may think that it is too great of a risk to hand over the control of your life to God. No one will force you; He will not force you. When you are ready, He will be there. He wants you to be on His team. And remember, He has predicted that only those on His team will win. That is something that you really need to think about.

Chapter 5
Understanding the Coach's Strategy

When we are living in a situation that we find oppressive, life can be difficult to manage. I have had times when I felt like the major parts of my day were filled with demands that I could not meet, some legitimate and some not. During my college days, work and school became a routine of pushing harder, being more accurate. In my situation it was necessary for me to remain in this high-stress position to get what I wanted: a good education and enough money to maintain financial stability.

Often we land in a tough position either by our own choosing or by circumstances out of our control. We find ourselves facing personalities and forces that we find very oppressive. A proper response is cry out to God and ask him to rescue us.

God possesses the resources necessary to end all oppressive situations in our lives. But the fact that God is able does not mean that God will do it—at least not right away. After all, God is not Superman; he is God. Superman flies down and beats up the bad guys. God, on the

He not only wants to deliver us from the evil villains; he also wants to rescue us from ourselves.

other hand, has a much more comprehensive deliverance in mind. He not only wants to deliver us from the evil villains; he also wants to rescue us from ourselves. We have much to learn before we can understand how to be delivered.

A good example of this principle can be found in the historical account of the Israelites that lived in Egypt under Thutmose III.

Thutmose III, a ruthless, tyrannical pharaoh, caused the people of Israel to become slaves. He treated them poorly and took advantage of them. The people cried out to God in pain.

Do you know what! Don't miss this point: *God heard them!* How many times have you cried out to God and it seemed like you were talking to the walls? No cavalry comes riding over the hill; no angel comes sweeping down and wipes out your enemies; no chariot comes and carries you away—at least as far as you can see.

What we find in the case of Israel vs. Egypt is deliverance "God-style." The strategy that God employed to gain the release of Israel was intended to teach both the oppressed and the oppressor. The lesson: freedom can only be realized when the heart and mind are released to the control of God.

So how did the story turn out? The oppressors (Egypt) either ended up killed by the angel of death or drowned in the Red Sea. The oppressed (Israel) died complaining in the desert. It does not appear that either side picked up on the lesson that God was trying to teach.

So what is the moral of the story? Call Superman, not God? I don't think so. After all, Superman is just as fictional as the notion that any of us are too good to be in need of instruction. We, like the oppressed in the story, have the opportunity to receive true freedom in a Promised Land. The only catch is that it might take a while, not for lack of power on God's part, but for lack of understanding on ours.

Chapter 6

What Kind of Player Am I—Really?

You owe me a debt, and you can never repay it.

You owe me a debt, and I am going to do everything in my power to make you repay. But you can never repay!

You owe me a debt, and I will never tell you what you owe me, but you still owe me, and you can never repay!

You owe me a debt, and my life will not be restored until you repay, and you can never repay! You sinned against me and you need to stop. That sin caused me harm. It took something from me that cannot be replaced. But God demonstrated his love for me and you in that while we were yet sinners, He sent His only Son to die to bring the forgiveness for my sins and yours. And His love has made my life complete without your repayment.

Therefore you owe me nothing. You have no debt.

It's very important to understand how you fit into The Game. How does a person qualify to be on God's team? Many people think, "I might have a slip-up once in a while, but overall, I'm a pretty good person." People who think this way tend to use those who commit murder or steal or commit adultery as the barometer for good and bad. There is always someone you can compare your life with who has committed more offenses, someone whose sins make you look good by comparison. This is not a new thought—people have thought this way for a long time.

Then God's Son Jesus came to Earth and turned everything upside down. He showed that a perfect life *is* possible. His perfection created two categories for good and bad: Him and us. There are no in-betweens; there are only people who have committed crimes punishable by eternal torture, on the one hand, and, on the other hand, Jesus Himself, who had committed no crimes. *None!* In the process, He eliminated the self-righteous argument that "there is always someone worse than I am."

We cannot qualify to play in God's game because we are fallen, sinful people. We don't like to admit it, but deep inside us we know that the ugliness that characterizes our inner being disqualifies us from being on the same team with a holy God. Jesus pointed out that even if you *think* of murder or adultery, you have committed that crime. Even if a human judge would not convict us, our own hearts know the truth and will convict us.

We cannot qualify to play in God's game because we are fallen, sinful people.

Any lawyer would have to admit that he has a solid case against us. That is what is so amazing about what Christ did. He embodied a concept that few really understand and many angry, offended people don't want to understand: forgiveness. John 3:17 says that he did not come into the world to condemn the world, but that the world through Him might be saved. He did not come as a judge, although He had every right to do so. He came with a gift to offer: Himself. He came to accept the punishment for anyone who wants to receive the payment. The only catch is that you have to realize that you need for the payment to be made by someone else on your behalf. In other words, we have to lay down our pride and take our rightful place among the thieves and prostitutes. Like them, our only hope is to accept the gift.

The result of accepting God's gift causes us to be reborn, free of debt, free to live as God intended. That is why, although my body has problems, my soul should not. That is why a prisoner can walk free within tall, imposing walls. That is why people who have committed great offenses against each other can forgive each other.

God's forgiveness has also given us a great example of how we ought to view each other and our faults. It helps us to be true teammates together.

Look at the way the Bible depicts the people it tells us about. The events of their lives are described as they are—with no cleaning up. There are no excuses, but neither is there a system of personal value based on mistakes they did or did not make. The sins of the past did not necessarily disqualify them from a changed, guilt-free life in the future. Paul murdered Christians, and because of this the leaders at the time decided he was disqualified. They did not realize that God had already approved of him.

We need restraints; we are prone to sin. But in our attempt to hold others accountable we need to make sure that we do no become twenty-first-

When our standards for forgiving others exceed God's, we then become the offender and the sinner.

century Pharisees. When our standards for forgiving others exceed God's, *we* then become the offender and the sinner.

When it comes to sin, there are two different groups of people. Those in the first group avoid sin to preserve their reputation, so that they will look good. The second group avoids sin because it is wrong. According to 1 John 1:10, everyone sins, so it is inevitable that on some issues both groups will fail and commit sin. The first group will likely feel shame or embarrassment, but the second group will feel the sadness which is the result of having failed a loving God who wants the best for his children.

Some offenses are more difficult to deal with than others. It may seem impossible to forgive some things. Many people could write an entire book describing the pain they have had to face. But we are crossing the line when we choose to compare sins and judge ourselves or others in a way that God has not done. In the end He will make everything right.

Look at the teachings about forgiveness in just one chapter of God's Word (bold emphasis mine):

"If your brother sins against you, go and show him his fault, just between the two of you. If he listens to you, you have won your brother over. But if he will not listen, take one or two others along, so that 'every matter may be established by the testimony of two or three witnesses.' *If he refuses to listen to them, tell it to the church; and if he refuses to listen even to the church, treat him as you would a pagan or tax collector.*

"I tell you the truth, whatever you bind on earth will be **bound in heaven, and whatever you loose on earth will be** *loosed in heaven."*

"Again, I tell you that if two of you on earth agree about anything you ask for, it will be done for you by my Father in heaven. For where two or three come together in my name, there am I with them."

"Then Peter came to Jesus and asked, **"Lord, how many times shall I forgive my brother when he sins against me? Up to seven times?"**

Jesus answered, "I tell you, not seven times, but seventy-seven times."

"Therefore, the kingdom of heaven is like a king who wanted to settle accounts with his servants. As he began the settlement, a man who owed him ten thousand talents[1] was brought to him. Since he was not able to pay, the master ordered that he and his wife and his children and all that he had be sold to repay the debt.

"The servant fell on his knees before him. 'Be patient with me,' he begged, 'and I will pay back everything.' The servant's master took pity on him, canceled the debt and let him go.

"But when that servant went out, he found one of his fel-

28

low servants who owed him a hundred denarii.[2] He grabbed him and began to choke him. 'Pay back what you owe me!' he demanded.

"His fellow servant fell to his knees and begged him, 'Be patient with me, and I will pay you back.'

"But he refused. Instead, he went off and had the man thrown into prison until he could pay the debt. When the other servants saw what had happened, they were greatly distressed and went and told their master everything that had happened.

"Then the master called the servant in, 'You wicked servant,' he said, 'I canceled all the debt of yours because you begged me to. Shouldn't you have had mercy on your fellow servant just as I had on you?'

Forgiveness—from God to us and from us to others—is the only path that can take us back to the original state of friendship with God.

In anger his master turned him over to the jailers to be tortured, until he should pay back all he owed.

"This is how my heavenly Father will treat each of you **unless you forgive your brother from your heart.**"
Matthew 18:15-35

Forgiveness is the only path that can take us back to the original state of friendship with God. Forgiveness is essential to understanding who we are and how we ought to treat each other. Without forgiveness from God, we cannot be on His team. Without forgiving others, we cannot be effective members of God's team.

[1] That is, a million dollars
[2] That is, a few dollars

Chapter 7
What Do You Really Want?

What do you want to accomplish in this game called Life? What really matters to you? Think through the decisions you would have to make in each of the following situations. What choices would you make? What do those choices say about what you value?

Money

Someone just walks up and hands you a suitcase with one million in cash. There's no catch, just a million in cash.

1. You could use the money carefully. Invest, make interest, and never work again.
2. Spend it all, forget about working, and go broke.

It's not unusual to think that our financial situation is the cause of all unhappiness. We are barraged by marketing professionals who spend a great deal of time and energy selling to us. Spending money has become a national pastime. The appeal of a bigger house and a more expensive car may bring some relief from the everyday pains of life, but buying for wrong reasons can only bring more pain and difficulty.

> Cash can bring relief from tangible problems, but it is limited in what it can accomplish.

Our financial needs are relative, aren't they? Cash can bring relief from tangible problems like paying bills and having a place to stay, but it is limited in what it can accomplish. It cannot bring tears of pride to your eyes like when your child takes his first step; it cannot bring comfort when you are hurting. It cannot replace the presence of a parent, or heal a broken marriage. Contrary to the claims of a popular credit card company, true happiness cannot be bought.

"Be not deceived—a man reaps what he sows."

Food and Clothing

A group of advertisers chooses you as model for life. You are guaranteed food and clothing for life.

Just go to the store and pick out what you want. No need to pay—you can go worry-free.

Would the challenge of finding bargains be gone? How much might you weigh? Would you have to continue to buy bigger clothes?

This book is about daring to believe. That means believing when things are bad as well as when things are good. Sometimes prosperity is more difficult than poverty. The worst thing that can happen to a person is to succeed and not be ready for it. This was what God warned Israel about in Deuteronomy 8:10: "When you have eaten and are satisfied, praise the Lord for the good land He has given you. Be careful that you do not forget…"

Health

You make an appointment with your physician for a physical. Following the examination your doctor determines that you are a candidate for a treatment that makes it impossible to contract any disease.

Your only concern: wearing out with old age.

Is health everything?

Although this is the exact opposite of what most people hear at the doctor's office, there will come a time and a place where there will be no more sickness and no more tears. There was a time in our lives when believing in a place like this was not so hard. Why have we allowed ourselves to be deceived into only believing what our five senses tell us?

Is there something more?

You are late for work. Living in Chicago, you should have known about the traffic at rush hour.

A prominent company employs you; your office overlooks the metropolis. You have your job because you try hard. You know how to make things work. As you sit and wait for traffic to move you notice a man, obviously underprivileged and probably unemployed. As you watch you can hear him shouting. You roll down your window to find out what he is saying.

" Take up your cross! Blessed are those who mourn, for they shall be comforted. If you wish to save your life, you must lose it. Consider it all joy when you encounter trials and temptations, knowing that the testing of your faith produces maturity."

This is all very confusing. You wonder whether you should follow this man and find out more.

Would you:
1. Ignore the stranger?
2. Choose to pursue a man like this and risk being miserable?

Guess what! If, intrigued by the strange call to pain and sometimes misery, you pursue this man, you will find the greatest gift anyone could ever give—a perfect life in exchange for an imperfect one. This man represents One who has the power to save life and be life—Jesus Christ.

"Whoever has the Son has life, whoever has not the Son has not life" 1 John 5:12.

You can fill up your life with things that promise happiness, or you can take a chance that God knows what is really good for you.

Every day we make choices. When I allow my three boys to play a total of seven sports in one season, the result will be a very busy three months.

The choice brings a lot of game-watching, a lot of transporting kids to practice, and a lot of coaching responsibilities.

When you face a difficult situation, you have choices to make. You can fill up your life with things that promise happiness, or you can take a chance that God knows what is really good for you. I had to make some decisions when I was diagnosed: give up, or fight. I have had to learn to fight it with God's help, because fighting it on my own is not possible.

In Parkinson's Disease, the brain sends messages through hair-like fibers. When an impulse is sent, it must jump from one nerve ending to another. In a normal person the brain produces a chemical called dopamine that will carry that impulse over the gap.

The Parkinson's patient does not have enough dopamine to enable impulses to jump from one nerve ending to another.

The Parkinson's patient does not have enough dopamine to complete that process. Therefore, treatment focuses on providing the brain with the dopamine that it needs. The side effects involve getting too much or too little stimulation. It is very difficult to regulate. To complicate things further, the brain has a blood barrier that prevents an easy route of medication to the proper area. You need medicine to get the impulse to jump. A medication called Synamet covers the synapse between nerve endings, helping it to jump over.

The problem is that as the disease progresses, the medication has more side effects due to the brain's unique structure and defense mechanisms. The results can be extensive amounts of dyskinesia, uncontrollable rapid muscle movement. In my case, the dyskinesia worsened when I was hungry, excited, or tired. It could make watching the kids play sports, coaching, or just performing routine tasks around the house an exhausting experience. The problem of freezing up made walking in crowds or going to a school function difficult. One Christmas program I had to sit by myself on the front row because I could not walk well enough to get to where my family was sitting. Eventually, I was forced to give up softball, quit playing tennis and basketball, and eliminate all the things I like to do to get exercise.

Although I got to the place where I could not run, I could still do pushups. That became my principal form of exercise. In fact, doing many pushups would sometimes help to get the medicine working.

It was very crucial for the medicine to work and help the impulse to reach the muscles. When you don't have any impulse to your muscles, it's not painful; but it's like what I imagine hell to be like. I found that no positioning would bring comfort to my body. I was just in total misery.

Jesus did a lot of healing during his ministry on earth. But his ultimate focus was on the hearts of those he touched.

It wasn't actual sharp pain; it was just misery—misery that you can do nothing about. The most relief I could find was to lie on the floor and pull my arms up against my chest until the medicine started working. Sitting up was just total, indescribable misery. Every muscle in my body was miserable. There was no escape.

Nights were the hardest for me. I would desperately need rest, but when I would lie down, my arms and legs would contract. One night, as I lay awake considering my choices, I sensed God asking me:

"Do you want to be healed?"

I responded, "Lord, do you think that I enjoy falling down, giving up softball, basketball, and tennis? Do you think that I like waking up night after night, not able to sleep? Do you see how it hurts to see my wife struggling with pain and anxiety and to feel my impact on my children slip as they have to play without me?"

He asked again, *Do you want to be healed?*

"What are you really asking, Lord?" I inquired. "I remember reading about the invalid Jesus talked with at the pool of Bethesda. A commentary I read suggested that an invalid of that day could profit greatly from being disabled. That explanation has to be made by someone who has never been an invalid. Of course he wanted to be healed!"

Yet God asked again, *"Do you want to be healed?"*

I wondered, "Could Jesus have been talking about spiritual healing, having to do with whatever sin He was referring to in His later meeting in the temple?"

Do I want to be healed?

Maybe He was talking about the difference between physical and total healing. When He healed ten lepers, only one gave thanks to God. The others were satisfied with just physical health.

Jesus did a lot of healing during His ministry on earth. But his ultimate focus was on the hearts of those He touched.

Like many of us, Simon Peter, a hardcore fisherman, found believing difficult. After all, he had made a good living for himself. He worked hard. He was responsible. He was in control of his life. Until he met Jesus.

Peter was fascinated with this man who called himself God. He was willing to give up a lot for him. But Jesus always seemed to want more.

Because Jesus was able to know the future, He was able to know that Peter would fail Him in His hour of need. Peter, who did not know the future, was sure that he would not.

When the predicted event occurred, Peter wept bitterly. Jesus had broken through. Peter, who had previously held his heart in tight control, let it go. Jesus made it through His great ordeal alone, and Peter learned that there is more to life than living.

Peter learned that there is more to life than living.

After Christ returned to Earth, he came back to find Peter. He knew that Peter had learned something, but He asked him a question so that we would get the point.

"Do you love me more than these?"

Peter answered: "You know all things. You know my heart. You know I love You."

Jesus asked again, *"Do you love me more than these?"*

"I love you," Peter answered.

"Do you love me more than these?"

"I give in. You have my heart, I believe that you are the one who is the author of life. I dare to believe in you!"

What happened when Peter gave up his control? I'll not give away the ending. Just read the second chapter of Acts, and the books of 1 and 2 Peter.

Chapter 8

Whose Timeline Am I On?

Deadlines. We all face them.

- "The store will be closing in 5 minutes. Please make your final purchases and bring them to the cash register."
- "You need to be at the field no later than 6:45, because the game starts at 7:30."
- "You have until October 17 to complete this report."

"You have a personal meeting with Jesus Christ, the Son of God, on __/__/__. Don't worry about being late—He will find you. But you do need to be ready."

God has been more than anything I could have ever dreamed He could be. If I fail, He comes through. People remind me of my failures; God forgets. The world measures success by prestige and things. God measures success by testing our ability to appreciate a sunrise. He sets the schedule—I don't.

When I am satisfied with my degree of maturity, God comes up with an event that is tough enough to crumble the foundations of my pride. He is not disconcerted with the mess that is caused by the process. He is only concerned with the outcome of His work.

God is not disconcerted with the mess that is caused by the process. He is only concerned with the outcome of His work.

Living with Parkinson's has changed my entire perspective of life. In one sense, you realize that life's short; God's in control and you're all right. On the other hand, you have to make it through every day. I have to figure out how to do that. I try to take on too much; I don't think quite as clearly as I should. I make plans, but never know if something's going to work or not.

There was the time that I was asked to speak at my nephew's graduation. I had prepared; I was excited. But when it was time for me to speak, I was lying on a cold floor behind the stage trying to figure out how I was going to reach the stage to speak. They delayed my speech as long as they could. When they could wait no longer, I got up and made a run for it. I don't know why, but sometimes I can run when I cannot walk. I jumped over the risers, ran to the podium, and held on. I gave my speech. After the speech I ran out the back, around the building, got into my truck, and fell asleep.

Another time I went to Cincinnati to a soccer tournament. Afterwards several families went to a restaurant to eat supper. As I was walking toward the restaurant from the car, my body quit working and I froze up. So I just sat there looking over the river. I sat there for almost an hour. I tried a number of times to get moving, but I could not take a step. Part of the problem with eating at a restaurant is that when I am hungry my symptoms worsen. Finally, after repeated tries, I somehow made a less-than-graceful entrance to the restaurant. Everyone else was almost done eating, and my food was cold. But I was still there—and I was still a part of my kids' lives.

When you have times like that, you do start learning to treasure the little things. You realize that your life may never be the way you dreamed it would be. But you also realize that God is doing a greater work in you.

When I see the results of His work in me, my greatest hope is that He does not quit working.

Over the years, I have experienced a few of God's remodeling projects. They have been quite painful. Yet when I see the results of His work in me, my greatest hope is that He does not quit working. The greatest possession we can bring to a meeting with God is evidence that we have been willing to let him work His magic in our lives. That will bring joy to His eyes on the day of our meeting.

"For we all must appear before the judgment seat of Christ, that each one may receive what is due him for the things done while in the body, whether good or bad."

2 Corinthians 5:10

Chapter 9
Does It Matter How I Play?

My diagnosis with Parkinson's disease was not the first event that required me to deal with God on a real basis. As I mentioned ealier, when I was a freshman in high school my grandparents were killed in a car accident. And when I was twenty-five my oldest brother died of colon cancer. These were very significant, life-changing events for me.

My life has always been kind of difficult—sometimes by choice and sometimes by circumstance. I had a September birthday, which made me always the youngest and shortest in my class. I graduated from high school and began my freshman year of college at age 17. I married at 19.

The responsibilities and the first-hand view of the brevity of life have combined to show me that the only real hope to be found is in God. No matter what happens in life, you have a choice as you react to it, and God rewards those who have faith in Him. He does not want us to put up an outward show that we trust him—he does not want us to fake it. If we struggle, he is more than willing to work with us. But it has to be real. If it is, you will know it.

When you look at the descriptions of God in the Bible, you will see a God who requires a lot, but who always gives much more than He requires. He always seems to wait until the most dramatic moment to come to our rescue. I mentioned before that my brother Tom died in 1988. He was a missionary to Mexico. Tom loved baseball and softball, so in his memory his best friend, Jim Beal, and Jim's brother Dick began a memorial tournament with area churches to raise money for mission projects in Mexico. We have faithfully hosted the tournament since his death. My other two brothers, Mike and Greg, along with myself and other friends, played on a team called Tom's Tigers. A couple of times we got close to the championship round, but for twelve years we were not able to win the tourney.

What happens when The Game really gets you down? Incredibly, that's your greatest opportunity to become a winner. Frank's story is an example:

> "Give me the phone," Frank demanded. "It has got to be the bank. I have been waiting for someone to call back about my consolidation loan."
>
> " I didn't know that you had talked to anyone about our finances. You know how I hate having everyone know how far in debt we are," chided Alice, his wife. At Frank's insistence she handed him the telephone.
>
> "Hello, this is Tom with National Loans," said the voice on the other end.
>
> "That's not who I called," Frank thought to himself, confused.
>
> Tom continued, "Your original loan company referred you to me. When I saw the situation that you were in I asked to take on your case.
>
> "What case?" asked Frank. "This is a debt consolidation; what could be so interesting about that?"
>
> Tom did not answer the question; he just gave Frank an appointment and hung up.
>
> Frank was a little confused, but he had so much on his mind that he dismissed the conversation and returned to his list of things to get done for the day.
>
> The next day, when Frank went for his appointment, he was a little surprised to find that the address that he had been given was the local courthouse. "What kind of loan agency has an office in the courthouse?" Frank wondered. Curious now, he proceeded to the meeting.
>
> After walking down a large hallway, and down two sets of stairways, he reached the dim, deserted-looking basement. A light was on in one office. Frank, now more than a little apprehensive about this loan officer, stopped at the closed door. Finally he opened the door, expecting to see a secretary. No one was there.

*Then Tom Dustin came out from a back office. He intro-
duced himself and greeted Frank warmly. Frank quickly
asked, "Am I mistaken? This seems like a strange place
for a loan officer to conduct business."*

*"I guess you do deserve some explanation," answered
Tom. "You have been under surveillance for some time. I
work for the President of the United States, and I've been
given the task of replacing the current financial advisor
in Washington.*

*"Your present financial situation will be our topic for
discussion, but you should know something. The invest-
ments that you made that caused you to go into debt were
actually brilliant, insightful, wise decisions. It took an incredible amount of manpower to make sure the companies
you invested in did not succeed. This was necessary to test
you. Our present advisor is about to be indicted for embez-
zling funds. The president wanted someone he could trust.
You have been chosen. You have maintained your integrity
despite the odds against you."*

Impossible, you say? Look in the Bible at the incredible true
stories of:

Joseph, who maintained his integrity. God brought him from a
slave and prisoner to ruler of the land of Egypt (Genesis 37-45).

David, who also maintained his integrity. God gave him the
kingdom of his enemy Saul—and even caused the Messiah to be
born as David's descendant (1 Samuel 16-2 Samuel 2).

Moses, who remained faithful and was entrusted with leading
millions of God's people out of Egypt to the promised land (Exo-
dus 3-10).

Daniel, who kept his integrity in the land of exile. He was used as
an instrument for answers to prayer for his people, and was shown
God's plan for the ages (Book of Daniel).

What about our team's discouragement over losing the memorial
game for my brother? Last summer we won three out of our four
games during the all-day tourney. This qualified us for the champi-
onships, which involved two more games. We won both. To some
this might seem insignificant, but I know my brother would have

been very excited. There were a lot of tears as the Tom Sharp Memorial Trophy was given to my mom and dad. You would have thought we had won the World Series.

And it was really strange when, for the first time after a hot August Ohio day, a strong breeze blew through the park.

You never know what God has planned for those who dare to believe.

You never know what God has planned for those who dare to believe.

Chapter 10
Playing in Bad Weather

How do you keep going when the storms of life come? That's when you realize how desperately you need a guide to get you through. The interesting thing about this game is that while the Creator does have final control over the circumstances, He still asks us to keep playing when He permits storms to hit.

Why does God allow our lives to be so difficult?

We just want to enjoy life. Yet at times it seems that each step brings more pain and suffering.

During my early years in church, a husband and wife musical team visited for a week of services. All that I remember is a song they sang called "Something Good is Going to Happen Today." It is very natural to expect life to be this way. But in reality, life often seems to resemble the symptoms suffered by those of us who have contracted an incurable disease. Incurable diseases have one thing in common: they get worse; they do *not* get better.

> **The Creator does have final control over the circumstances, yet He still asks us to keep playing when storms hit.**

The symptoms of a difficult life can involve a number of circumstances. Our daily routines can be set into turmoil by financial decisions, such as mergers, reorganizations, or cutbacks, that are out of our immediate control. Our personal safety can be threatened by natural disasters like tornadoes, hurricanes, or earthquakes. The variety of problems that a person can encounter is as diverse as the lives that can be led, involving anything from family problems to issues of national security. The challenges that some must confront can be overwhelming. The anesthetics commonly prescribed by our world do not work.

The typical response to a world like this is to endure each day longing for answers, yet afraid to ask any questions. We are afraid to ask for fear that the answer might cause even more pain.

Can we possibly understand the Christian life and the sometimes-confusing plan? People have been asking these questions about the difficulties of life for a long time. When Jesus Christ came to earth claiming to be God, crowds of people gathered to get some answers. He never seemed to feel any pressure to defend Himself or his Father. His responses typically confused His audiences. In most instances, He answered the questions that people did not ask, rather than the questions they were asking.

His answers even confuse those who really do want to serve Him. His battle plan in the cosmic battle of good and evil was unveiled as He held an infant gently in His arms. He spoke out to those desperate for relief from their difficult political, religious, and economic climate. What did He tell them? "If you want to find the wisdom of time and eternity, become like the infant that I am holding, for the kingdom of heaven is made up of these."

We have to admit that although our own ideas sound good and seem to make sense, they do not work.

They must have said, "Huh?"

Like the people Christ spoke to that day, we feel that the way to handle pain and confusion is to get tougher, work harder. We look for some way to eliminate the source of the pain.

So what is God saying to those who suffer?

Maybe He is saying that there is another way to live than we have known. Could there be a way that enables any person, in any situation, to manage life successfully?

We may be confused by Christ's description of the successful life. Yet we have to admit that although our own ideas sound good and seem to make sense, *they do not work.*

48

We are left with few real options. We can complain and be un-happy with our lives. Or we can learn what God is trying to teach us.

What *is* God saying to those who suffer?

He is saying that we cannot enter the kingdom of heaven with-out His help. We may be able to get close, but if we do not accept His help, we will never make it. However, if we become like little children we can cry (to God), fall down, and get back up. We will not be overwhelmed when we don't understand everything, because we will trust that God our Father does understand, and that He has everything under control.

If we remain young at heart we realize that we have a lot to learn—and compared to God's age, we're always going to be young and learning. We will keep learning in a way that will never change for eternity in the kingdom of heaven.

What is God saying to those who suffer?

"*Trust Me.*" That's all He needs to say.

Chapter 11

What if I Can't See Where I'm Going?

The Christian life can be described as a venture in faith and trust. We don't always have a clear road map.

It can get scary when life gets crazy: kids, occupations, growing older, change, good adventures, bad adventures, stepping out in faith. It's scary living life on the edge without anesthesia, battling an enemy who claims to be a friend.

We regularly travel the road that is comfortable. Seldom do we willingly choose the high road, the one that goes way up where we have never been before, where God can speak to us. But by choosing the comfortable road, we miss out on the adventure, and we miss out on the chance to see what our God can really do.

By choosing the comfortable road, we miss out on the adventure, and we miss out on the chance to see what our God can really do.

Micah described well what following God involves. If anyone requires more than what you read in the next statement, they are not speaking for God.

> *He has showed you, O man, what is good.*
> *And what does the LORD require of you?*
> *To act justly and to love mercy*
> *And to walk humbly with your God.*
> *Micah 6:8*

A good example of trusting God can be found in Joshua 3:1-4.

It was an event that began, as all good adventures do, early in the morning.

God had a journey that He wanted his people to take, a different route that they were not familiar with. God said, "Trust Me, and you will know which way to go."

Why was it so important that they trust Him? Why is it so important that *we* trust Him? Because we have never been this way before.

In Joshua 3:1-4 we find these instructions: "Get ready, because tomorrow the Lord will do amazing things among you."

He asked young and old alike to cross a huge river at flood stage! It's a great illustration of the way God works:

- He showed them the way.
- He provided the training necessary to accomplish the task.
- He comforted their fears of failure by guaranteeing success.
- He took care of the miraculous intervention required for success in the mission.

What did *they* have to do? They just had to step into the water.

I don't know what raging river God is calling you to step into, but if he asks you to make the step, He will do his part to equip and protect you.

They just had to step into the water.

I was officially diagnosed with Parkinson's disease in the fall of 1991. When my wife and I first got the news of my Parkinson's, it was pretty overwhelming. My thoughts were jumbled and confused. While I felt some relief in having a name for my problem, I was very uncertain what the future would hold.

I did not question God right away, but the idea of contracting an incurable brain disease at the age of 31 was not very encouraging.

Outwardly I had to appear optimistic so that my family would not panic. Inside, however, I was and still am unsettled as I face the strength of this powerful disease. After all, life is difficult enough with a body in good health.

It is a constant struggle to maintain faith when there does not appear to be reason for hope. Yet there *is* a reason to hope. The Apostle Peter learned that lesson. He learned that through all the pain and disappointments, something good can occur.

"Since Jesus went through everything you're going through and more, learn to think like him. Think of your suffering as a weaning from that old sinful habit of always expecting to get your own way. Then you'll be able to live out your days free to pursue what God wants instead of being tyrannized by what you want.

I Peter 4:1-3 The Message

Peter is another good person to speak to the issue of faith, because he had some challenging encounters of his own with the Son of God. In one particular encounter, Jesus came to his boat during a storm, walking on the water. Peter had so much faith in God that he left the safety of the boat and stepped onto the water to go to Jesus. As long as he kept his eyes on Jesus, the storm and the size of the waves were irrelevant. If you know how the story ends, you know that when he took his eyes off Jesus, the storm suddenly became very relevant. He began to sink, and had to cry out to Jesus to help him.

My attitude toward life in light of my illness has been quite similar to Peter's experience. As long as I keep my eyes on Jesus I can walk on water; if I look away, I sink.

Fortunately, God understands our weaknesses. He can use whatever faith we do have to accomplish something good. Our lack of faith does not please him, but due to His great love, God finds only one kind of person unforgivable: the person who thinks he needs no forgiveness.

What I did not know when I was diagnosed in 1991 was that God was preparing an amazing answer for me. Three years earlier, a doctor performing a brain map on a Parkinson's patient mistakenly touched an area of the brain that caused the patient's dyskinesia (which is involuntary, rapid muscle movement) to cease. The doctor apologized. But the patient was thrilled, because the "mistake" had relieved his symptoms. It was the beginning of a new approach to treating Parkinson's.

I am not saying that if you believe enough, God will take away all suffering. Many do not see the answers to their prayers until heaven.

What I *am* saying is that God can be trusted! I do not hold the position that God will heal all our sicknesses here on earth. And there has to be something important about asking God for help.

Do you ever remember reading that he turned down someone who asked him for healing?

Jesus did not heal everyone on earth when he was here, but do you ever remember reading that He turned down someone who asked Him for healing? Just something to think about.

Chapter 12
Scouting the Opponent

Whatever your position on the team, there is an opponent out to get you. He will pose as a guide; he will try to deceive you. He is a ruler, but only because God permits him to exist. He will do whatever he can to prevent a move toward God and away from the world order that he now controls.

His name is Satan. He once knew the kindness of the loving God and was even part of the forces of good. He was an angel. In Luke 10:18 Christ talks about how Satan fell from heaven, and Isaiah 14:14 explains why. Satan had looked at his own power and beauty and deduced that he could equal God. He failed to acknowledge that all he was and had came from God.

Satan is a very formidable enemy, but he is far from invincible.

Satan is a very formidable enemy, but he is far from invincible. In fact, he has a number of weaknesses. Here are a few of them.

He is ignorant: Before Christ came to earth, a number of prophecies had been made concerning his life, death and resurrection. Let's just pick one—the prophecy that no bone would be broken on his body, despite the fact that it was the custom for crucifixions of that day. If Satan wanted to discredit God, all he had to do was read what God had said, then tell the soldiers to break Jesus' leg. Satan blew a real opportunity! Did he not have the power? Or did God blind him? Whatever the reason, it makes him look like what he really is—powerless in the face of God.

He has no future: Since Satan does not have a future; he is left with only the present to offer. That's how he tries to deceive people—he uses the philosophy, "Live now, have pleasure now, do not worry about the effects on the future." He fails to add, "Because in my world there is no future."

He has no creative power: Satan is not able to create; therefore, he and his forces must depend on perverting what God has created. To counter healthy marital sex, for example, he pushes control, pornography, abortion, etc. His version of leadership involves domination, hate, coercion, and deception. To counter God's plan for healthy interpersonal relationships, Satan promotes a demanding spirit, superficiality, and emptiness. Satan is happy when we are not looking for a relationship with God, and he has many temporary substitutes to keep us deceived until it is too late.

He is no ultimate match for God: No matter what Satan does to mess up our lives, he does not have the final say. If your life is extremely difficult due to circumstances beyond your control, do not credit Satan. He can only mess up your life to the degree that God allows. Do not blame God; for whatever reason, He has allowed your difficulty. It somehow fits into the whole plan for the forces of good and evil. God does have the right to ask you and me to endure present difficulties for two reasons:

1. God has provided the example of enduring through hard circumstances by dying on the cross that should have been ours.
2. God does have a future to promise.

If you are too afraid, because of your present situation, to take a step toward God, remember that anything that keeps you from coming to God is a deception of Satan. Don't fall for your opponent's strategy. No matter what things look like on the surface, it is God who will ultimately win.

Chapter 13
Defeating the Opponent

If you are a part of God's team, you will have to battle Satan. He will do everything he can to draw your attention away from being effective on God's team. As the Bible describes it, we are divided, like a horse with a bit that has two ropes pulling two different ways. Due to God's grace we're in the Book of Life; but if we keep letting Satan draw us away from what God is trying to do in us, we are saved "as by fire." That does not sound like it would merit a hero's welcome.

Keep in mind that there are only two ultimate forces that lead men on this earth: God and Satan. Satan's only hope is to deceive us through lies. You don't have to look far to see how lies can destroy lives, families, friends, trust, and anything else they touch. Unfortunately, many people choose to rationalize or be deceived rather than accept the truth. So whenever you do something that you have to lie about, it might be wise to think about whose idea it actually was.

Truth, on the other hand, is so valuable that Jesus was willing to live, die, and come back to life for it. What He knew before He came to earth was the truth about the future. He knew that after three days He would rise from the dead. He knew that He would be revisiting the earth to

Truth is so valuable that Jesus was willing to live, die, and come back to life for it.

begin a new kingdom—a realm with no term limits, no democracy, no happy ending—just happy times and no ending.

Jesus held to truth throughout His time on earth. Despite repeated

57

attempts by Satan to beat Christ at *Truth or Dare*, the Bible never records an incident where Jesus lost, or lied, or hesitated to answer the challenges. He claimed to be perfect and did not need to be ashamed of, or hide, anything.

Undefeated at *Truth or Dare*—that is a claim that none of us can ever match. But whether we are Christians (which means our name is in the Book of Life) or not, we all live by some standard, or set of rules. If rationalizations, deceptions, or selfishness are a part of our accepted rules for conduct, the Bible tells us that we deserve to be condemned along with Satan, the father of all these lies (Romans 1).

Overcoming Satan's strategies involves learning to live by the truth.

Jesus was so committed to living truthfully that He was willing to face pain by choosing to live in the world our deceit had infected.

The last week of Christ's life on earth was more than eventful. Most everyone has heard of the suffering and pain he had to endure. Although I am sure that the physical abuse was very difficult for Jesus to face, it is the emotional pain that really broke His heart. And it was the rejection of His claim to be the Son of God that made it impossible for Him to extend forgiveness to many people.

The people that witnessed Jesus' last days found different ways to say "no thanks" to an offer from God for a new clean heart and a bright future.

The religious leaders of the day said, "He must be silenced, as He is messing up our status as the rule-makers!"

The Roman leaders made fun of Jesus, mocking His claim as King of the Jews, saying He was irrelevant. The followers of Jesus hid and were ashamed to be asociated with Him. Sound familiar? We have not learned much in two thousand years. Everything is much the same now as it was then. Many religious leaders are making many rules for people to live by that result in dead ends and chains that inhibit life. We have public policies that make Christianity (followers of Christ) irrelevant to the social and economic stability of our culture. We who follow Christ are afraid to tell people the truth. He who has Christ has life; he who does not, has not life. It has been said that those who do not learn from the past are bound to repeat it. What will it take for us to stand up for the truth and live like Christ did?

Overcoming Satan's strategies involves learning to live by the truth. We must choose, just as Jesus did, to only allow truth in our lives. The following chart has been included to help explain the emotional progression from a life built on lies to one of truth. Obviously, living by truth is not easy, but it is the only way to really be free and happy. It's sort of like my football coach used to say "You do not play the game to have fun; you play the game to win—and when you win, you will have fun."

This graphic illustrates our progress toward truth:

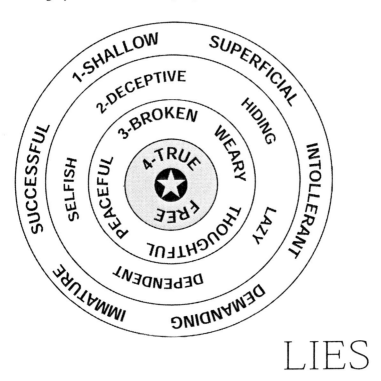

The outer circle represents a person who lives by a lie, without realizing the power it has over his or her life.

The next circle shows a person trapped and controlled by lies, one who understands the problem but is powerless to escape.

The third circle demonstrates a person on the way to freedom, in pain from giving up the security of quick fixes and temporary fulfillment, but beginning to feel alive for the first time.

The fourth circle is the Free Circle. It is best described with names: names like Abe Lincoln and great men and women like him, people who sacrificed personal satisfaction for greater causes outside themselves. Christ, who called himself the Truth, said, "the truth shall set you free."

The Free Circle is where heroes live. They are people who have learned that true enjoyment come not from personal comfort but in self-sacrifice for others. They are people who call sin, "sin," and who back their words with a life that can be respected. They are people so consumed with the Cause that nothing can detour them. They are the ones who defeat the opponent. They are people who choose to believe Truth.

To get to the truth we are going to have to believe. The Bible has repeatedly claimed that God is capable of meeting our every need, but if we never take him up on his promise and give Him a chance to act, we will never know what He can really do. We will never get to the Promised Land.

If we never take Him up on his promise and give Him a chance to act, we will never know what He can really do.

What is the Promised Land all about? It's about not giving up. It's about reaping what you sow when what you planted was good. It's about trusting in the God who makes big promises to come through when the odds seem insurmountable. It's about growing up and realizing what is important. It's about taking a stand for truth.

It is that moment when you feel invincible. You have trained hard and you feel ready for the challenge.

The Promised Land is made up of people who work through their problems and learn from them, who are too busy tearing down this world's strongholds to notice the injuries they have incurred.

They see something no one else can see.

They are motivated in a way that is supernatural. The Promised Land is where God is—because if God is there, Truth will be there, and Satan will have no foothold.

Chapter 14
Storm Warnings

"If you have plans to be out today, forget them; we are expecting a severe weather system to be passing through our area."

Weathermen—they are a very important part of our daily lives. They have highly technical equipment capable of forecasting future events. Some have gotten so good that they have a five-degree guarantee, giving out prize money if their forecast is wrong by more than five degrees.

The information from those who forecast the weather can be critical to our safety.

"Hurricane Henrietta will be moving ashore. Evacuation orders have been issued."

"A tornado has been spotted moving into this county. Take shelter in a safe place, either in a basement or inside wall away from any windows."

"We can look for 8-12 inches of snow, blowing and drifting with temperatures well below zero. If you do not have to go out, do not. If you do, be very cautious; the storm is powerful and the roads are drifted, icy and treacherous."

God, like the weatherman, has predicted the future. However, unlike the weatherman, He does not need to offer prize money if He is wrong. He has never been wrong, and He will never be wrong.

He predicted a flood during Noah's time. He predicted the death and resurrection of his Son. He predicted the return of Israel as a nation.

The predictions God has made that have not yet been fulfilled involve everyone's future. He has predicted the return of His Son, a final world war, and a new kingdom—a kingdom led by his Son, one that will never end. It will be a kingdom where all people past and present will submit to His judgments. If He was right before, what are the chances He will be right again?

Weathermen base their predictions on scientific principles that have proven to be true in the past. The exact sequence of events can only be estimated.

When you look at your life as you expect it to be next week, you have no way of knowing what awaits you, good or bad. Yet we all hang on to life as if we really have control over it! When our future becomes unmanageable, we pull together all our resources to handle it.

We all hang on to life as if we really have control over it!

We gain a false sense of security—and a personality that is compulsive and anxious—as a result of trying to be something that we are not.

Those of us who claim to believe in the future that God has predicted need to be careful not to live like we are trying to make things work on our own. We can all tell stories about how we believe in God and His great kingdom; we can argue with atheists about the existence of God. We can prove that evolution is a hoax. But until our belief causes us to examine our lives and align our heart and will with His, we cannot claim to believe in God. James says if any man hears the word of God and does not do what it says, he is like a man who, after looking at himself in the mirror, walks away and forgets what he looks like.

I have found that it really does not matter what I say if my life does not reflect the content of my speech. If God's Son really is coming back, it ought to make a difference in how we approach our lives. Yet most times it does not.

Knowing the future has its advantages, and also its responsibilities.

Growing up in my home involved a lot of physical activities. I had three brothers, and a sister who was and still is a great cheerleader. We liked to do a lot of things together. One activity we loved was playing football in the living room. Naturally, this was not something Mom and Dad permitted. We wanted to play, so sometimes when they were not home we would play anyhow. I remember the urgency we felt to clean up our mess when it was time for them to come home.

Once Mom and Dad came home early. Suddenly playing football in the living room did not seem to be nearly as much fun. We had made a big mistake.

If we read that the Creator is coming back to judge and we do nothing to prepare ourselves, we are making a big mistake.

If we read that the Creator is coming back to judge and we do nothing to prepare ourselves, we are making a big mistake.

Chapter 15

Playing in a Looney Tune Life

The kindergarten teacher walks into the room. The students are out of their seats, making an incredible din. At the teacher's command the children return to their seats and cease their activity. They become quiet as the teacher begins to read. "Once upon a time... in a small village long ago...."

We all love a good story, especially the ones where the good guys win, or where someone performs an amazing feat, or stories that include any number of plots that we find entertaining.

There's nothing wrong with stories, but we need to watch how they affect the way we play The Game. For many of us, our lives have been filled with perfect worlds and perfect endings—not in real life, but on the television screen. Most shows on television have a plot which can unfold and be resolved to the satisfaction of the writer and viewer in an hour or two—sometimes in thirty minutes! In the looney tune world of cartoons, characters are flattened by huge boulders, run over by cars, electrocuted, and shot. And they're back for the next scene!

When we read in the Bible that we will reap what we plant, do we find it hard to accept?

What does viewing this type of entertainment do to our thinking? When we read in the Bible that we will reap what we plant, do we find it hard to accept?

Jesus shared a story that carried a far different message than our cartoon fantasy friends. His story is real life. It is a story about two construction workers.

The first one found a good site to begin his building. He chose

67

carefully a rock-solid area to build his house. He left nothing to chance. He built his house by following good building practices and all the proper building codes.

The second builder had watched too many cartoons. He figured it did not matter where his house was built. He owned a piece of land near a beautiful lake. Since he wanted to be close to the water, he built his house on the sandy shore.

Soon both houses were completed. Both builders occupied their new dwellings with a sense of accomplishment. However, it was not long until a huge storm came up. The wind blew and the rain pounded on the houses. Since this is a real-life story, you can probably predict the ending. After all, everyone knows what happens when you build a house without a proper foundation.

Every time we sin, we are building our lives on sand.

Or do we really know? Every time we sin, we are building our lives on sand. Yet we still do it! What are we looking for in our lives? Where are we looking to find the satisfaction of our needs? We are constantly called to choose: God or entertainment, God or money, God or career. We have to battle a heart that we cannot trust as we search for a foundation that can stand up to reality.

When hard times come, I think of the Rich Mullins song:

> *"Hold me, Jesus, 'cause I'm shakin' like a leaf. You were then king of my glory; won't you be my prince of peace?"*

Do we always feel in control, confident and together? No. Is that required to serve God? No. It's a good thing, because there are many times when I have felt that I could not make it through another night. After a busy, stressful day, I would come home and be on the go until time for bed. I would fall asleep quickly, but fifteen minutes later someone would come into the bedroom needing something. Once awake, I would be awake for three hours. I tried music, baths, watching Jay Leno reruns, doing pushups, reading, writing—nothing seemed to work. Sleeping pills make it hard to get started the next day, so I try to avoid them. Praying is hard at that point—I tend to have a bad attitude when I have gone without sleep. My middle son, Jordan, once made a statement that described these nights well. He said, "It's always dark at night."

Yet somehow, when I was at my worst and could not even pray, someone must have been praying. The morning always came, and the problems of the night seemed so much smaller then. We don't need a cartoon life to be able to overcome the struggles of life.

Can God handle our problems? We need to give Him a chance to do so by building our lives on a solid foundation.

Chapter 16
Can I Make It?

One day in 2000 when I visited my doctor, he explained that I was at a point in the progression of my Parkinson's disease where I could no longer function normally, even with medication. He suggested a new option: brain surgery. Because of my condition and all the difficulties, I had become a candidate for a new procedure called Deep Brain Stimulation. The procedure had been used with patients in Europe for ten years, and they had not had a return of the Parkinsons' symptoms.

Some of those close to me were very excited about the possibilities. I wasn't too sure. Was this really an option? Ten years ago, who would have of thought that I would be choosing between a body that does not work properly and *brain surgery*? In the pre-operation consultation, I was warned of pain and agony, and possible death. With all the fun I had been having, what did I have to lose? I agreed to the surgery.

I realize that although I did not like the thought of brain surgery, for many the hope of improvement does not exist at all. You may have contracted circumstances that appear to be irreversible. The cause of pain can vary dramatically from one person to another, but the actual feelings of fear and anxiety are universal. Sometimes The Game takes us to places that we would never chose, and we certainly would not want to go alone.

I was thankful for the many people who strengthened me along the way. My co-workers gave me a "good-luck" party, with cake and everything. I had been involved in a Bible study group since before my diagnosis. The group met specially that week to pray and anoint me with oil. It was very touching. I could not have asked for any closer friends all huddled around me asking an incredible God to allow a miracle to take place.

My sister sent me a care package. It was carefully prepared, with dates for each gift to be opened. Each gift included something encouraging, along with a Bible verse. One example of the contents of this well-conceived package was the gift I unwrapped one day containing little green "army guys." A verse was included, reminding me to "put on the whole armor of God, that you may be able to withstand the attack of Satan." The gifts ranged from an Operation game to a tennis pen. I was in great anticipation for what she would have on the last day before surgery. To my surprise, she had managed to find a Six-Million-Dollar-Man game (fortunately for my insurance company, the surgery did not cost quite that much!).

It is amazing how some people are able to see others in pain and insightfully plan ways to encourage. I have found that whenever I feel a burden to do something for someone, it needs to be done. That voice might just be the voice of God.

The night before my brain surgery I looked for something familiar to help me deal with my apprehension of the following day. Not only was I having brain surgery, but I would be awake throughout the seven-hour procedure!

God had made some promises to me that I could hold onto for the next day—and for the rest of my life!

As I looked in the Bible, I found an old, well-known psalm: Psalm 23. There I found that God had made some promises to me that I could hold onto for the next day—and for the rest of my life! They are available for you, too.

I found these three assurances that can comfort anyone who wants to walk with God:

1. You are with me! (v. 4). Not only was God with me, but He provided many loving and caring people from all over the place: family, friends and churches. Many people were praying for me. *That night I was far from alone!*

2. You can defend me from anything (v. 4). "Thy rod and staff

comfort me." God is my shepherd and He has the power to take care of me no matter what, no matter where.
3. Enemies do not intimidate God (v. 5). He prepares a feast before me in the presence of my enemies. Whatever or whoever stands in your path as a challenge is no challenge to God.

I said there were only three points to make, but one other point could be relevant here. The whole valley of the shadow of death thing is an exception to the lying down in green pastures and walking by still waters. So hold on tight—maybe the roller coaster ride will end and you can get off!

Psalm 23

The LORD is my shepherd, I shall not be in want.
He makes me lie down in green pastures,
He leads me beside quiet waters,
He restores my soul.
   He guides me in paths of righteousness
      For his name's sake.
Even though I walk
      Through the valley of the shadow of death,
   I will fear no evil,
      For you are with me;
   Your rod and your staff,
      They comfort me.
You prepare a table before me
      In the presence of my enemies.
   You anoint my head with oil;
      My cup overflows.
Surely goodness and love will follow me
      All the days of my life,
      And I will dwell in the house of the LORD
         forever.

Your life may not have turned out exactly how you imagined:
-The perfect house and the perfect marriage.
-Kids who just love to be with you.

-Dream vacations whenever you want to take them.
-Good health.

But with God's help, you *can* make it through victoriously.

Chapter 17
Moving Past the Line

In this game, how you started doesn't have to affect how you finish. The following three scenarios are taken from the history of three public figures. Can you tell the names of these three individuals?

#1 was born on a bed of poles covered with cornhusks. His father was an uneducated carpenter and farmer. His mother had little or no schooling but could write. His younger brother died in infancy—his mother died when he was nine.

#2 was desperately eager to be part of the adventurous life of her older siblings and terribly envious of her sister's nonconformist image. She wanted to be like her, to be a dashing law-breaker, but didn't have the proper instincts or the courage, and was always scorned for passively going along. Where her sister was the rebel, she followed the rules. She was Goody Two-Shoes, begging to be taken along with her brother and sister wherever they went. They considered her a pain.

#3 lived on a small farm with a strict father who required him and his siblings to finish schoolwork and farm chores. When he was seven his family moved off the farm, and he had more time to play his favorite game: cowboys and Indians. He also began attending a monastery. He took part in the boys' choir and was said to have a good singing voice. This young boy idolized the priests and for two years considered becoming a priest.

The past is not always a good indicator of the future.

These childhood beginnings have been included to illustrate that the past is not always a good indicator of the future. Even the same home can produce quite different results. Everyone knows about the ruthless Al Capone, but not everyone knows that his brother was a presidential bodyguard and a sheriff. How many times has the one voted most likely to succeed in high school actually done so? On the other hand, if my high school English teacher finds out that I have written a book, she will probably have to sit down for a while to get over the shock!

Trusting God allows His power to transform your life. When you consider following Him, hang on—He has all things at His disposal. The more of your heart you give to Him, the crazier—and more exciting—your life is likely to become.

The more of your heart you give to Him, the crazier—and more exciting—your life is likely to become.

The day before my scheduled brain surgery at Cleveland Clinic, my wife, my father-in-law, and I took the four-and-a-half-hour trip to the clinic. My father-in-law volunteered to drive, taking away any opportunity I might have to turn back.

I did not get anxious until we got to the Cleveland city limits. My wife had thoughtfully taped a message by Chuck Swindol on the topic of anxiety. He read a poem from Tim Hansel's book *Holy Sweat* that I found very comforting. I'm including it for you. It reminds us how far we can move if we put the right Person in charge of our lives.

The Road of Life

At first, I saw God as my observer,
my judge,
keeping track of the things that I did wrong,
so as to know whether I merited heaven
or hell when I died.
He was out there sort of like a president.
I recognized his picture when I saw it,
but I really didn't know Him.

But later on

when I met Christ,
it seemed as though life were sort of like a bike ride,
but it was a tandem bike,
and I noticed that Christ
was in the back helping me pedal.

I don't know just when it was
that He suggested we change places,
but life has not been the same since.

When I had control,
I knew the way.
It was rather boring,
but predictable...
It was the shortest distance between two points.

But when He took the lead,
He knew delightful long cuts,
up mountains,
and through rocky places
at break-neck speeds,
it was all I could do to hang on!
Even though it looked like madness,
He said "Pedal!"

I worried and was anxious
and I asked,
"Where are you taking me?"
He laughed and didn't answer,
and I started to learn to trust.

I forgot my boring life
and entered into the adventure.
And when I'd say "I'm scared,"
He'd lean back and touch my hand.

He took me to people with gifts that I needed,
gifts of healing,

acceptance,
and joy.
They gave me gifts to take on my journey,
my Lord's and mine.

And we were off again.
He said, "Give those gifts away;
they're extra baggage, too much weight."
So I did,
to the people we met,
and I found that in giving I received,
and still our burden was light.

I did not trust Him,
at first,
in control of my life.
I thought He'd wreck it;
but He knows bike secrets,
knows how to make it bend to take sharp corners,
knows how to jump to clear high rocks,
knows how to fly to shorten the scary passages.

And I am learning to shut up
and pedal
in the strangest places,
and I am beginning enjoy the view
and the cool breeze on my face
with my delightful constant companion, Jesus Christ.

And when I'm sure I just can't do anymore,
He just smiles and says, "Pedal."
                    —author unknown

If you think a relationship with God will result in an unfulfilled life, you must be looking at people who are only pretending to trust God. I have found that God is not satisfied with pretense. He has gone on record as saying that either by choice or by judgment, every knee will bow to Him. We have a choice to voluntarily bow to Him now or bow to Him at the Judgment later. This message is not popular today, but His power and truth have a way of eliminating popular terms like "politically correct." Only a message that is really true can help us make sense out of life.

If you think a relationship with God will result in an unfulfilled life, you must be looking at people who are only pretending to trust God.

So it doesn't matter where we started. What matters is where we go. And where we go depends on who we allow to be our guide.

Two of the childhood examples cited in this chapter exemplify the power that is available to those willing to trust God with their lives. Example Number One was destined to free many people. This gift that he gave changed our country forever. He spoke the immortal words: "Fourscore and seven years ago our fathers brought forth on this continent a new nation, conceived in liberty..." President Abraham Lincoln made choices that changed the course of our nation.

Number Two married one of the greatest evangelists to ever live. Ruth Anne Graham, wife of Billy Graham, has played a part in the eternal freedom of millions.

What about the third example? Although he had a better start than many, he did not finish well. His name was Adolph Hitler.

Whom we choose as a guide, and what we choose to believe, is what makes a difference—not how we started.

Chapter 18

Small Miracles?

"I need a miracle!" How many times have we heard someone say that?

Before discussing this topic, I want to explain that the use of the word "miracle" in this context does not fit the typical theological definition of the word. Theologically it is used of an occurrence of supernatural origin and character, such as could not be produced by natural agents and means. But many things could *possibly* be produced by natural agents, yet are not necessarily *probable*.

Walking up to my hospital room the night before surgery, I remember wondering what the next twenty-four hours would be like. I had prepared myself for a painful day and a miraculous recovery. The painful part began when I bypassed my final dose of medication at 7 p.m. This does not seem to be a real problem until you consider that I had not missed a treatment in ten years. The disease had progressed to where I was taking five different medications four times a day.

I slept about an hour, then woke up to a body reaction that I had not encountered before. I had wondered how bad I had gotten—now I was finding out. I fought to find a comfortable position. My left arm began to cramp. The cramping got so bad that my wife had to get up in the middle of the night, come to my room, and massage it. This task would eventually be continued throughout the surgery by one of the operating room nurses. I do not know if I could have survived the cramping without this dedication.

When the night was over, morning was welcomed, with a few reservations. A little naive, I remember telling the nurse when she arrived that it had been an awful night. I knew I was in trouble when she said in an emotionless tone, "That's about normal."

She took me to a lower floor to get a haircut and a real nice crown.

Then I was transported to another room for a brain scan.

Following the scan I was taken to a waiting area. By this time my arm had become painfully cramped, and they were not able to reach Kelly to come help me. It's strange what you think about during times like this. I kept thinking about the many things that had been invented and discovered over the years. If I had this disease or syndrome five hundred years ago, what would my life have been like? I would probably lie in bed in agony day after day.

I was in great pain. I was extremely fatigued. And I had not even gotten to the difficult part yet!

Although I had experienced a lot of pain and discomfort, the surgery was a new lesson in endurance. Although it is not unusual for a surgeon to inflict wounds on a patient for the purpose of correcting some problem that cannot be accessed in any other way, the surgery to implant the Activa Deep Brain Stimulator is different, because the patient gets to be awake and alert during the wounding!

It is necessary (they tell me, anyway!) to remain alert in order to respond in ways that would allow the computer technicians, surgeon, and all the supporting staff to guide a small fiber from a hole drilled in the skull down a long path through the brain's vital compartments into a small area only microns in size. The process involves moving the wire, then testing the hand and leg for dexterity. Then it needs to be moved again and again, until the desired results are achieved. What I couldn't figure out was, "Why should such a simple task take all day?"

I soon found out why. During the surgery, a neurological specialist kept moving my fingers, hands, arms and legs as the neurosurgeon moved the wire through my brain. Whenever the neurosurgeon hit the correct area in my brain, my movements would create noise in the background on the computer, and the doctors would know that they had found the correct area for the stimulator to be placed.

The surgery, like any surgery, had its difficult moments. But all quickly faded in significance when the surgeon and his team were able to guide that small wire to the microscopic location in the hypothalamus area of my brain. I knew they had found it, because for the first time in ten years I could relax my arms. The cramping immediately disappeared. Strength was restored and dexterity returned. I was still attached to a computer, and would still need to have two stimulators implanted in my chest the next day, but the worst was over. And there are some advantages to being awake. The surgical staff tried to take a break after their work on the right side of my brain before starting to work on the left side. I told them I was miserable, so they did not stop. I probably saved myself at least fifteen minutes!

The next day two wires from my brain were attached to two pacemakers that were implanted in my chest. I could turn them off and on with a large magnet.

Within two weeks I was able to walk, run, and play games.

This miracle was performed with the use of sophisticated technology, implemented by an extremely talented staff at the Cleveland Clinic. I owe them greatly for my new life. The great thing about this stimulator is that if a cure is discovered some day, the stimulator can be removed and does not damage the brain.

If a miracle could be defined as "God doing something spectacular," could there ever be a small miracle? The big ones like parting the Red Sea or feeding the five thousand are great, but what about the ones where God uses the expertise of one hospital team or one corporate group to affect one person?

In my mind miracles can only remain small if those involved in the miracle do not give credit to the their ultimate source, the spectacular God! When a miracle is seen for what it really is, everyone it touches and everyone who asks God for it feels the impact of God. When we feel the impact of God, we can understand why life is not really life without Him.

How many people actually get to see a miracle?

I am beginning to train to run in a mini-triathlon.

I have had the opportunity to write.

I have been privileged to see God at work in ways that could not be possible without my disease. I saw God care for my family by providing employment at just the right time. I experienced the skilled hand of a surgeon and an exceptional team of assistants who were able to accomplish what few have done: reversing the symptoms of a degenerative disease.

Although the power that I can demonstrate on my best day is next to nonexistent, God's power has no measurement or limitation. Yet His power is available to anyone. Anyone who can survive the staggering intensity of his strength can have use of it. Just ask and it shall be given unto you. Above all else, remember not to ever give up. Miracles can still occur, so no situation is ever over.

Mark was awake during the entire seven-hour surgery so that surgeons could determine the correct position for the wires to his brain.

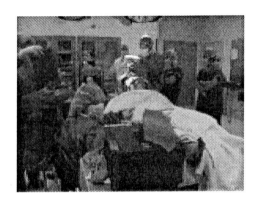

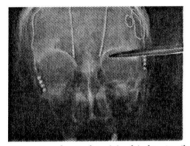
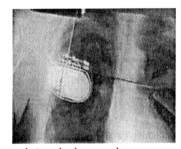

Wires implanted in Mark's brain (left) send signals that can be controlled by pacemakers in his chest (right).

A few days after surgery, Mark could drink coffee and read at the same time!

Chapter 19
The Things That You Just Have to Do

Sometimes you feel like you must do something a little extreme! For example:

Distance swimming: English Channel swimming captured the popular imagination in the second half of the 19th century. Captain Matthew Webb of Great Britain was the first to make the crossing from Dover, Eng., to Calais, France, in 1875; his time was 21 hours 45 minutes. The map distance was 17.75 nautical miles (33 km), but the actual distance of a Channel Swim is frequently lengthened by tides and winds. By the 1990's successful crossings had been made by swimmers as young as 12 and as old as 65. Various swimmers had crossed both ways with only brief rests between the swims.

Dangerous Races: The Iditarod dogsled race course crosses two mountain ranges, runs along the Yukon River for 150 miles (241 km), and crosses frozen waterways, including the pack ice of Norton Sound.

Mountain Climbing: Alison Hargreaves, a British mountaineer, died in a blizzard while descending from an apparently successful assault on the Himalayan peak K2 only weeks after she had become the first woman to scale Mt. Everest alone and without bottled oxygen.

Sky Diving at Terminal Velocity: Terminal velocity is the steady speed achieved by an object freely falling through a gas or liquid. A typical terminal velocity for a parachutist who delays opening the chute is about 150 miles per hour.

Why risk possible drowning to swim the English Channel? Why compete in the Alaskan Iditarod race and face the daily risk of freezing temperatures? Why climb Mt.Everest or the Himalayas and risk death? Why would a skydiver want to delay opening the parachute to achieve terminal velocity?

History has recorded numerous examples of men and women compelled to accept great challenges. What kind of person would take such risks? What can be learned from this group of adventurers?

Here are some observations that may help us understand the need some people have to accept new challenges.

1. They are self-motivated people just looking for a worthy challenge.
2. They are able to get the best use of the abilities given to them by God.
3. Fear does not control them—it motivates them.
4. Failures only raise their level of determination. They do not know when to quit.
5. Long and tedious preparation is tolerable and necessary. They accept it as part of the process.
6. They think differently.
7. They are not the majority.

Something that I felt I had to do was run in a triathlon. One just happened to take place only seven months after my brain surgery. (My mom was praying that I would not participate!)

Attitude is something that God holds higher than any victory in any event.

The event consisted of a quarter-mile swim, a twelve and a half mile bicycle ride, and a three-mile run. You who have competed in Ironman races probably do more than this just to warm up. Remember, though, that the point is to get the most out of the abilities God gives us. This event was definitely a stretch for me.

I think it is important to notice those playing team sports who work hard at practices, maintain a good attitude, and rarely get to play. Then when finally given a chance, they give their very best effort. These people are the ones who really get the maximum use of God's gifts, because attitude is something that God holds higher than any victory in any event.

I trained for about a month and a half before the triathlon. I read what I could about how to train for such an event. I trained at whatever part of the day I felt the best. It was difficult at first, but it got easier as I pressed on.

When the big day came I was a little nervous but I felt ready. The competition began with the swimming. A rope extended from the beach out to a pontoon boat docked an eighth of a mile offshore. The 350 swimmers would be required to swim around the boat and back. As I stood in the water near the beach, I couldn't believe that an eighth of a mile could look so far away.

Many times we commit ourselves to something, like quitting smoking or sticking to a diet or a budget, or taking some difficult step in a relationship. We have great intentions, but when we stand on the beach and measure the price we're going to have to pay, it can be enough to make us want to turn and run away.

The gun sounded and the race began. My inexperience became quickly evident. The combination of eating too much breakfast, nerves, and medication left me out of breath and nauseated.

Again, this a is typical reaction to facing difficult odds. There is probably a good reason why we avoid our personal challenges. I am sure that David felt a little sick when he listened to Goliath laugh at his sling and five stones. The big thing to remember when situations get tough is that if it is something you're supposed to do, God will bring you through it. It may not be pretty, from a human standpoint, but it will be accomplished.

My swim was the most difficult part of my race. I had to stop and hold the rope several times, and I finished the swimming with the police divers following me. Does that sound like

I regret the many times in my life when I knew what I needed to do and did not stand up to the pressure.

success? It all depends on what you are trying to accomplish. My goal was to finish. That is what I had to do. I am sure the winner of the race wanted to win, and that's what he had to do.

The rest of the race went well and I even finished under two hours. When it was all over I felt great, because with God's help I was able to meet a very intense challenge. It makes me regret the many times in my life when I knew what I needed to do and did not stand up to the pressure.

Hebrews 12:1 says it well,

"We'd better get on with it, strip down, start running and never quit." —The Message

Running the Triathlon

Mark comes out of the water after the swimming part of the triathlon. The outlines of the pacemakers that control his deep brain stimulators can be seen on his chest.

Mark drops to his knees after crossing the finish line.

(Photos by Gary Nieter)

Chapter 20

Am I missing something?

The final whistle blows; a winner is determined. A group of tired, dirty contestants celebrate. The hard work and skill displayed by the team have proved to be enough to put them in the winners' circle. They experience the satisfaction that makes all the sacrifices worthwhile.

Winning brings with it recognition and awards. Times of victory become the highlights of our lives, and often our accomplishments become standards by which we measure our lives. Why is it that during times of great happiness we ask the hardest questions—questions like, "Is this as good as it gets?" or "Why do I always want more?"

Why is it that during times of great happiness we ask the hardest questions?

It is vacation time and the tourist attraction site of the day is Niagara Falls. For those who want to get a glimpse of the beautiful falls, a viewing deck is available safely on the opposite shore. The view is a quite amazing.

When you ride the boat under the falls, however, it becomes truly awesome! Somehow the incredible force of the water changes all perception of the power of that waterfall.

As a father, I have never gotten over the incredible miracle of the birth of my sons. But if I don't continue to be aware of and impressed with the work that God continues to perform in them, then I have missed something.

Winning, appreciating beauty, and making room for God in our lives all have one thing in common. They all make us aware that we are missing something—that we are not yet complete. It is our vision for the future that helps us understand how we ought to view the present.

When we attend an awards assembly, there ought to be an enjoyment of victory, but also the anticipation of the day that will be "as good as it gets." There will be a day that will satisfy completely.

As Jesus said, "You have not seen anything yet."

The difference between seeing something like a waterfall from far away and up close is the difference between seeing heaven from earth and being there. The fact that God has done great things in the past is true. But we can't be satisfied with just remembering what God has done. As Jesus said, "You have not seen anything yet."

Chapter 21
Finishing Well!

I could say that God has promised what we all want—deliverance and a life free from trouble. But the easy life hasn't always proved to bring happiness.

I could say that life would be difficult to the end, so get prepared. But while it may happen that way, we can only handle a future like that one day at a time. We are better off not knowing that information.

I could say that our true Promised Land is in heaven and we ought to live on that basis. This *is* a fact, but I have not met anyone yet who looks forward to the trip there.

The final chapter is supposed to be positive and upbeat and provide all the answers. But... when I began working on this book, my intent was to only write about concepts that I really believed. Based on that, I will have to be honest and tell you that I am still searching for the end of this book.

I am now recovering from a surgery that may actually keep my disease in check. Many of you have not been so fortunate and still remain in situations of great pain and difficulty. All I really know is that no matter what situation we find ourselves in, and no matter how little **God cannot be controlled, manipulated or quantified.** or how much we understand about our lives, it is critical that we allow God to provide our solutions. The process of surrendering our lives to God is a difficult one. Listening to Him and following Him can be mysterious and complicated at times. He does not use conventional methods of communication. He cannot be controlled, manipulated or quantified. He speaks to our hearts through the Holy

Spirit. He speaks through others who are active in relaying God's message of love.

He is God!

These verses contain the essence of what I have learned about God and the benefits of a relationship with Him.

> *However, as it is written:*
> *"No eye has seen,*
> *no ear has heard,*
> *no mind has conceived*
> *what God has prepared for those who love him"*
> *I Corinthians 2:9*

> *But because of his great love for us, God, who is rich in mercy, made us alive with Christ even when we were dead in transgressions—it is by grace you have been saved. And God raised us up with Christ and seated us with him in the heavenly realms in Christ Jesus, in order that in the coming ages he might show the incomparable riches of his grace, expressed in his kindness to us in Christ Jesus. For it is by grace you have been saved, through faith—and this not from yourselves, it is the gift of God— not by works, so that no one can boast. For we are God's workmanship, created in Christ Jesus to do good works, which God prepared in advance for us to do.*
> *Ephesians 2:4-10*

> *So do not throw away your confidence; it will be richly rewarded. You need to persevere so that when you have done the will of God, you will receive what he has promised. For in just a very little while, He who is coming will come and will not delay."*
> *Hebrews 10:35*

> *But my righteous one will live by faith.*
> *And if he shrinks back,*

I will not be pleased with him. "
Hebrews 10:38

    But we are not of those who shrink back and are destroyed, but of those who believe and are saved.
Hebrews10:39

    Now faith is being sure of what we hope for and certain of what we do not see. This is what the ancients were commended for.
Hebrews 11:1

    By faith we understand that the universe was formed at God's command, so that what is seen was not made out of what was visible.
Hebrews 11:3

In the end, the true winners are ones that make the right choices in life. I ran across a poem that demonstrates a good example of what winning really is.

Hero of the Race

I saw them start, an eager throng
All young, and strong and fleet;
Joy lighted up their beaming eyes,
Hope sped their flying feet.
And one among them so excelled
In courage, strength and grace
That all men gazed, and smiled, and cried:
"The winner of the race."

The way was long , the way was hard;
The golden goal gleamed far
Above the deep and distant hills—
A shining pilot star.
On, on they sped, but while some fell,
Some faltered in their speed;
He upon whom all eyes were fixed

97

Still proudly kept the lead.

But ah! What folly! see, he stops
To raise a fallen child,
To place it out of danger's way
With kiss and warning mild.
A fainting comrade claims his care,
Once more he turns aside;
Then stays his strong young steps to be
A feeble woman's guide.

And so wherever duty calls,
Of sorrow or distress,
He leaves his chosen path to aid,
To comfort and to bless.
Though man may pity, blame or scorn,
No envious pang may swell
The soul who yields to love the place
It might have won so well.

The race is o'er. Mid shouts and cheers
I saw the victors crowned;
Some wore fames's laurels; some love's flowers
Some brows with gold were bound,
But all unknown unheeded stood—
Heaven's light upon his face,
With empty hands and uncrowned head,
The winner of the race.

One Thousand New Illustrations
Rev. Aquilla Webb, D.D. LL.d
New York, 1931

Life moves fast. One moment you are bragging to your friend that your mom and dad have ten thousand hundred dollars and you are looking forward to your first T-ball game; the next moment you're attending your retirement party. You can't afford to go through life alone. Your heart and soul will not survive unless you dare to believe. You will lose at the precious game of life and your defeat will be senseless. Why? Because there was a day that the game's creater rocked the heavens by declaring a bold plan. The announcement was made, "I will allow my son to be sacrificed in their place. He must live a perfect life, be a perfect substitute. This will stand as payment for their sins. Those who accept this payment will find the victory they were created for and their sins will be remembered no more. Those who do not must face my judgment, for I am a holy God, and sin must be hated and punished."

You can't afford to go through life alone. Your heart and soul will not survive unless you dare to believe.

As a result of God's plan, you and I have a decision to make. It is a decision simple enough that a small child can make it, but tough enough that many adults cannot.

The options are:
      Believe and win...
          ...or lose.

"For God so loved the world that he gave his one and only Son, that whoever believes in him shall not perish but have eternal life."
John 3:16

Printed in the United States
862900002B